Stoddard Glass

STODDARD FLAG FLASK. Two views of the same flask, showing at the l
the flag with 13 stars and 9 ridged stripes; the pole extends almost to
base on the left side. At right, on the obverse side, the embossing re
"New Granite Glass Works—Stoddard, N. H." The flask is a blood-aml
half-pint size, with a sheared top and open pontil

On the Trail of

Stoddard Glass

by Anne E. Field

William · L · Bauhan · Publisher
Dublin · New Hampshire

Library of Congress Catalog Card No. 73-153379
ISBN: 0-87233-021-4

Photographs by Joseph Binko

MANUFACTURED IN THE UNITED STATES OF AMERICA

To

all those who helped
in the preparation of this book
and to
collectors of historical glass
everywhere

Contents

Illustrations

Foreword

THE COLLECTIBILITY of Stoddard glass is derived not only from its form, color and texture but from the fact that bottles and other glass objects are literally a reflection of their times and the people who made and used them. Thus, this book, directed to collectors of glass, may also be of value to those interested in a brief and personal account of a uniquely combined art form and industry of nineteenth century New England.

Its aim is to provide a short history of the town of Stoddard, New Hampshire and glass-making as it flourished there from its inception in 1842 to its sad demise in 1873.

The book focuses on a description of the manufacturing methods in the local mills of that period and some of the people involved, with simple guidelines for identifying its products and photographs illustrating an ample range of Stoddard ware. I have not attempted to include monetary valuations, as they are subject to change from season to season. Accurate price information can be readily obtained from current antiques magazines.

It is hoped that by the use of local color and anecdotes

passed down through succeeding generations, a true image of this once lively little town has been evoked and its important contribution to the arts of America placed in proper perspective.

I would like to express my thanks to all the people who made this book possible. I am indebted especially to the following New Hampshire friends: the late Stephen Chase, Sr., and Mrs. Chase of Bennington; Mrs. George Fish and Mr. and Mrs. Chris Kernozicky of Keene; Mr. Roland Sallada of New Boston; Mr. Clifford Baldwin and Mr. and Mrs. George Chamberlain of Jaffrey; and Mr. A. Harold Kendall of Surry, New Hampshire.

My appreciation also goes to Miss Kay Fox of the Keene Public Library for her aid and advice; to Mr. Joseph Binko of Keene, who photographed nearly all the glassware shown here; to Joyce Williams and Jean Shepard for their assistance in the preparation of the manuscript; and to Mr. John M. Foster of Marion, Indiana, and the Currier Gallery of Art, Manchester, New Hampshire for their kind permission to reproduce photographs.

Finally, I would like to thank Frederick A. Williams, Jr. of Winchester, New Hampshire, who helped me to originate this book and aided in its research and compiling.

ANNE E. FIELD

Stoddard Glass

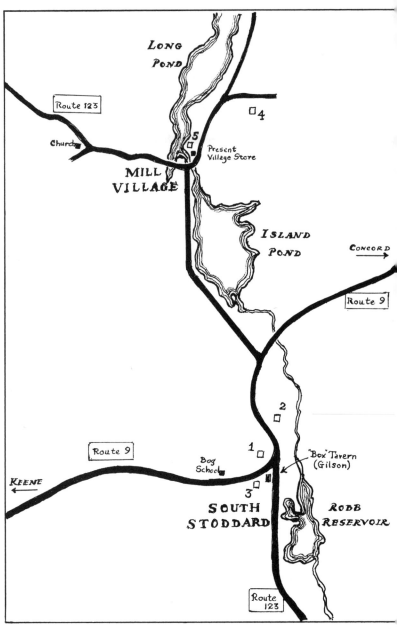

MAP OF STODDARD showing approximate locations of the glassworks:
1. Joseph Foster's first furnace; 2. Joseph Foster's second furnace; 3. South
Stoddard Glass Co. (Weeks & Gilson); 4. Granite Glass Co. (Curtis);
5. New Granite Glass Works

1

Old Stoddard

The Grand Old Hills in this location
Like sentinel guard on all creation
From bold summits looking down
As watch towers o'er our native town,
What transport now the vision fills
To see again Old Stoddard Hills.

In this verse taken from a poem written for the Old Home
Week Association Picnic in August 1899, Nellie Louise Whitney lovingly describes the little town of Stoddard, New
Hampshire which became noteworthy for its manufacture of
glass.

Earliest recollections record Stoddard as an inhospitable
wilderness in 1768 when its first settlers, John and Martha
Taggart arrived. The Taggarts, who had emigrated from
Londonderry, Ireland, endured untold hardships during
these early years, intensified by long and fiercely cold winters
with endless snowfalls. It is said that the well in the back
of her husband's shop was dug by Mrs. Taggart with her fire

shovel and that the first plow ever used there was carried by Taggart on his back from Peterborough.

Stoddard lies amidst the granite hills of southwestern New Hampshire, its rugged terrain, once cleared for pasture by the early settlers, now heavily wooded with second-growth pine and hardwood. The township is dotted with ponds and its most prominent natural feature is Pitcher Mountain (2153 feet), lying to the north of the present villages. About fifteen miles to the west is the fertile Connecticut River Valley, and to the south is the region's most celebrated landmark, Grand Monadnock Mountain.

It was from Mount Monadnock that Stoddard took its first name when it was chartered in 1752 as "Monadnock Number 7", one of a tier of wilderness townships so-named during the administration of the provincial governor, Benning Wentworth. It was—and is—one of the largest townships in area in this section of the state. Later, for a time, the town was called Limerick in honor of Scotch-Irish grantees.

In 1774, on the eve of the Revolution, Stoddard was incorporated and received its permanent name—six years after the Taggarts had made their settlement. The town was named for Colonel Sampson Stoddard, a surveyor and a veteran of the Indian Wars. Colonel Stoddard, who was a native of Chelmsford, Massachusetts and a graduate of Harvard, had been commissioned by the provincial government to survey much of the land in southwestern New Hampshire. For his services he received large land grants in the region, but he never came to live in the town that bore his name. He died in 1777.

The first houses in Stoddard were built of round timber; the chimneys and fireplaces were of stone and the ovens

16

were typically detached from the houses in the cause of fire protection. The Taggarts were followed three years later by the Richardson family, and by 1774 Stoddard had twenty-four inhabitants, but by 1780 the town had grown so rapidly that it was divided into ten school districts accommodating approximately 275 scholars. The first schoolhouses were built in 1792. The earliest public highway through the town was built from the southeast from Hancock and Peterborough, and within a few years another road had been built from the county seat at Keene. In 1822 the first post office was established under Isaac Duncan's aegis as Postmaster, and the mail was delivered by Peter Jacobs, who used a one-horse sleigh in the winter. In the next decade Captain Jonathan Sanderson put up a large tavern which later became known as the Central House and then the "Red Hotel." And a few years later Gilson's Tavern, or the "Box Tavern" was built at South Stoddard.

The town flourished during the early 1800's. It's population in 1790 was 701 people, and by 1800 it had grown to 1148, the largest number Stoddard ever attained—larger even than Keene's population at the time. The opening of rich farmlands in the west lured men away from New England, and the population of Stoddard, like other towns in the area, gradually dwindled. (According to Gould's *History* the population was 1105 in 1850, but the census of 1970 recorded only 233 people in Stoddard.)

But before its decline, Stoddard experienced a brief and prosperous renaissance, brought about by the burgeoning of its glass industry. Beginning with the Foster works at South Stoddard in 1842 and the larger factory at Mill Village in 1846, glass manufacturing continued for thirty years. At one

17

The Central House, Stoddard Village. Also known as the "Red Hotel," built in 1833 by Capt. Jonathan Sanderson. It did a thriving business in the olden days on

time over 800 persons were employed as blowers, firemen, carry-off boys, woodsmen and helpers. So involved was the general population, that women and children in nearly every home in town were engaged at this time in encasing the large jugs in rattan to protect them in shipment.

Ox carts made daily runs to Milford, by way of the "turnpike" through Hancock and Peterborough, loaded with fragile cargoes of amber and greenish glass bottles of every size and shape. From Milford they were shipped to Boston, there to be distributed to manufacturers all over the country, since it was known that most of the rare and best amber glass blown in America came from the Stoddard Mills.

Stoddard had in abundance the two things necessary for the manufacture of glass during the middle of the nineteenth century: clear fine sand and plentiful timber. Indeed, one bank of sand used, south of the old Route 9 contained the exact proportion of manganese to give the glass its famed olive-greens and ambers, while oxide of gold was also present to produce the beautiful red-amber color in other lots. The dark bottle glass was obtained by adding ashes and ground bone to the sand.

The thick forests of Stoddard easily supplied the enormous amount of timber necessary for burning to create the 1200 degree temperature required to melt the sand. In fact, the number of persons employed gathering wood was about as large as the number employed in the factory, especially since the wood had to be dried for about a year before it was ready for use in the furnace.

Glass made at Stoddard was usually ordinary bottle glass, but most always distinctively in olive-ambers, olive-greens and ambers which ranged from clear light amber to a deep red amber, sometimes called "blood" amber. However there also was a small amount of pure green glass manufactured there.

By 1870, glass manufacturers elsewhere had begun to experiment with the addition of new chemicals to the potash and sand mixture, and soon were able to produce clear glass. Due to this and the fact that gas and coal were now being used for fuel, the hand-blowing and wood-burning glass works became too expensive to operate, and the glass-making industry at Stoddard gradually collapsed.

The failure of the Stoddard Glass Works meant unemployment for hundreds. Many drifted to the glassworks at South Lyndeborough, New Hampshire and to New York state and other locations to practice their trade. By the turn of the century, with the loss of the glassworks and the allied slowdown of the lumber business, Stoddard went into an economic decline.

Today, though there is not a trace of the wooden warehouses and hexagonal factory buildings to mark the locations of Stoddard's once-famous glassworks, the beautiful hand-blown glass on the shelves of private collectors and antique dealers across the country stand as a tribute to the four factories at Mill Village and "Stoddard Box" that brought fame and prosperity to the little town of Stoddard.

2

Glass-making Comes to Stoddard

THE VERY FIRST GLASS was made by nature in volcanoes. It is called obsidian or volcanic glass and was used for spearheads and arrow tips by ancient man. The first man-made glass is attributed to the Egyptians c. 4000 B. C. in the form of beads and glaze-on-clay figures. The art of glass-blowing was created by the Sidonians, who produced jugs, free and hand-blown flasks, cups and dishes in many shapes. It was further developed during the period of the Roman Empire, when bottles and vases were skillfully blown and glass became an article of trade. The glass-making city of the Middle Ages was Venice, and the product of this era remains noteworthy for the magnificent color the Venetian glassmakers were able to achieve, especially in goblets and vases.

The next major step in the history of glassmaking was the window pane. Since it was far more difficult to flatten a bubble of glass than to blow the various shapes and designs described, there were delicately beautiful glass vases and objects before window glass came into being. The earliest window glass, therefore, was to be found in churches due to the expense and difficulty of its production.

Thus, for centuries, glass was scarce and costly. Every piece was made meticulously by hand in a time-consuming process, while the training of a skilled glass-blower was an equally expensive operation.

Glass is made mostly of sand, and it was undoubtedly the rich deposits of sand at Stoddard that first drew Joseph Foster and others to set up their glassworks there in the mid-nineteenth century. It may help us to remember that transparent glass is produced by mixing the opaque sand with soda ash, lime, lead, or a similar chemical substance to make it melt when heated. Making glass is somewhat like making candy. The sand is the sugar. The chemical that makes the sand melt takes the place of water that dissolves the sugar. Adding different kinds of materials makes the different kinds of glass, just as flavorings are added to make different kinds of candy. The mixture is cooked until done. Then it can be made into any shape wanted. There is, however, one big difference between making glass and making candy. The mixture for glass-making must be extremely hot in big furnaces. Clay pots must be used as iron ones would not stand the heat. There are, of course, many, many recipes for candy. There are even more for glass! The count exceeds 20,000.

Making glass is not as simple as first supposed. Very pure materials must be used to assure a quality product. Tiny bits of impurity may spoil a batch of glass. On the other hand, the addition of metallic oxides (which may be naturally present in the sand, or added by the glassmaker) gives to the glass its various and luminous colors. Just a tiny trace of iron-oxide, for instance, will give glass a greenish color. Another talent in making glass is to see that the glass cools properly. The mirror of the giant Palomar Telescope needed a whole year to cool.

The first important glass factory in America was established in Salem County, New Jersey in 1739 by Caspar Wistar, a Philadelphia craftsman, and produced fine hand-blown bottle and window glass, known as Wistarberg. Another eighteenth-century glass manufacturer was the famous Heinrich Wilhelm Stiegel, the German-born entrepreneur who built up a highly successful glassworks in Pennsylvania. Stiegel Glass was comparable to the best European glass in quality, but Stiegel went bankrupt before the Revolution and his skilled glass-blowers, most of them Germans, dispersed.

The glass made by these men was all hand-blown, as was all the glass produced before the nineteenth century. It was either free-blown—that is, blown from the end of a blowpipe by the breath of the glass blower—or blown-in-the mold—that is blown against the sides of iron molds.

But when Enoch Robinson and Deming Jarvis, in 1827, found a way of pressing glass into shape in a mold—as opposed to blowing it—glassmaking was revolutionized, and less costly glass for the populace was on the way. Robinson, a carpenter at the New England Glass Company in Cambridge, and Jarvis, owner of the Boston and Sandwich Glass Company at Sandwich, Massachusetts, took out patents for their pressing machines—in which a mechanical plunger pressed the glass into a mold and stamped it with a pattern. Thus, pressed glass, or Sandwich Glass, became enormously popular during the last century. Another radical change in glass manufacture was to come long after the Stoddard mills had come and gone. In 1899, a bottle-making machine was invented by Michael J. Owens. These machines account for the smooth mass-produced glass we know today.

Probably the earliest glassworks in New Hampshire was the shortlived enterprise at Temple, a small village about twenty-five miles southeast of Stoddard. Robert Hewes of Boston established the operation in 1780, during the Revolution, and hired Hessian and Waldecker glass-blowers who had been mercenary soldiers in the British Army. But fire and insufficient capital combined to close the works in less than two years. Except for fragments, there are almost no authenticated examples of Temple Glass known today.

A direct antecedent of glass-making at Stoddard was development of the industry at Keene, New Hampshire in the early years of the nineteenth century. The real founder of the Keene glassworks was Henry Rowe Schoolcraft, a soldier, author and graduate of Union College, who was born in Watervliet, New York in 1793 and came to Keene about 1814. From then until about 1855, glass manufacturing flourished in Keene. Two factories were built, the first on Washington Street, and the next year Schoolcraft built another on Marlboro Street. Their output was mostly window glass, but they also produced bottles, inkwells, decanters and tableware. Keene is probably most famous for its fine whiskey flasks, decorated with eagles, Masonic emblems, relief heads of the presidents, and other historical embellishments. Erwin Christianson writes in *The Index of American Design* (New York, 1950), "American drinking habits in the early nineteenth century . . . hastened the development of our glass industry. The price of whiskey was low, and the competition keen; it was the bottle that sold the product."

Two other glassmaking centers in the 1800's were Suncook and South Lyndeborough, New Hampshire. A factory was established at Suncook near the Merrimack River in 1839 but lasted only for about a decade. The Lyndeborough Glass Works was founded in 1866 and continued for about twenty years.

In the meantime, glassmaking was to commence at Stoddard. The first glassmakers to come to Stoddard migrated there from Keene—only fifteen miles distant—after the failure of the Marlboro Street Glassworks in 1841. As the Stoddard industry gained momentum, unemployed glass workers drifted in large numbers to nearby Stoddard, and it was in this remote town that glassmaking in New Hampshire was to make its mark between 1842 and 1873.

3

The Glass Houses of Stoddard

FOUR DIFFERENT GLASS HOUSES were located in South Stoddard and in Mill Village between 1842 and 1873. These settlements were about two miles apart. Mill Village was located to the north, where the present center of the town lies. South Stoddard, or "the Box", is only a highway crossroads today, where the present Route 9 and Route 123 from Hancock intersect. The name, "the Box", was applied to the odd-shaped four corners and to the old Gilson Tavern which stood on the spot for years. Another name for it was "The City", which gives some indication of how busy "the Box" was while the glass factory was in operation.

The four houses were:

1. Joseph Foster's, South Stoddard, 1842-50
2. Granite Glass Company (Curtis) Mill Village, 1846-62
3. South Stoddard Glass Company (Weeks and Gilson) South Stoddard, 1850-73
4. New Granite Glass Works, Mill Village, 1860-71

At full production, the last two mills ran night and day for about six months a year (due to the terrible winters), employing about 200 people. Wages were approximately four to eight dollars per day and somewhat more during rush periods. It is said that a skilled glassblower could make as much as twenty-five dollars per day. Women earned thirty-five cents apiece for making the wicker shipping covers—a day's work consisting of five or six. Many of the workmen were Irish or German and had come to Stoddard from Keene and Connecticut.

Joseph Foster's Works
South Stoddard

Joseph Foster, the founder of Stoddard's glassmaking industry, was already thoroughly trained in the art and manufacture of glass when, at the age of forty-one, he came to South Stoddard. He and his sons were to remain closely tied to the industry for most of its thirty-year existence. Born in England in 1801, Foster was trained from his earliest youth in glassmaking, and as a young man he emigrated first to Canada, and then to New Hampshire, where he settled in Keene. A Keene directory published in 1831, shows Foster as a glass blower at the Marlboro Street works, and about ten years later he purchased the company himself. In the meantime, he married a local girl, Mary Sanders of Fitzwilliam, and produced a large family of four daughters and six sons. The Marlboro Street Glassworks, it will be remembered, had been founded by Henry Rowe Schoolcraft in 1815, but by the time Foster acquired it, the firm had passed through a succession of owners and apparently been plagued by one financial crisis after another. Thus in 1842, undoubtedly hoping to improve his chances, Foster moved the entire operation fifteen miles northeast of Keene, to Stoddard. Here he bought property at the south end of the village, near the famous Stoddard "Box."

Very little is known of his endeavor, except for the brief account given in Gould's *History of Stoddard*. This dates Mr. Foster's arrival in Stoddard at 1842, at which time he "built a furnace, principally of stone in the old house west of Gilson's Tavern," ran it a short time, but having no capital, the long distance carting of the finished product consumed his profits and he failed. Although in 1849 Foster was still operating, and is listed in the *New England Mercantile Directory* of that year, by 1850—having again built another furnace 80 rods north of the village—he had failed once more and was forced to close the plant. Whiton and Curtis then took over the furnace and ran it in conjunction with the Granite Works. As we shall see, however, this was not the end of the Foster family in the history of Stoddard glassmaking.

Black glass bottles were made at Joseph Foster's Works. Other known products were a reddish amber one-quart bottle with the initials "F s" (the "F" in upper case and the "s" lower case); Masonic flasks, urn and cornucopia flasks (with an "x" on the side), Benninger types with banded tops, blacking bottles, demi-johns, and jars. These bottles were made in various colors of amber-green, olive, honey and reddish amber.

Of interest is a typical expense sheet from "Old Bottle" Foster's records:

Thursday, June 11, 1848, South Stoddard, N. H.

One Master Shearer-board himself	1.50
One wood drier-board himself	1.67
Two shearers of furnace boarded	.67
One material burner board himself	1.00
One mix in make 15.00 a month and boarded	.80
One Bottle Packer ovens	.80
One Empty ovens	.80
Five boys to carry off bottles	2.50
25 bushels of ashes	9.00
3½ bushels of salt	2.62
One bushel of sand	.75
For blacksmithing of tools, etc.	1.00
For blowers work—blowing 10 groce Sarsaparilla	16.80

GRANITE GLASS CO. OR C. CURTIS & CO.
MILL VILLAGE

In the meantime, a more successful business venture, the Granite Glass Company, also known for a time as C. Curtis and Company, was established in 1846 along the high bank of a small stream on the south side of the Antrim Road by Calvin Curtis, Gilman Scripture and John Whiton, Jr. The three partners also ran the Village Store and were all important men in the community. Scripture, in fact, was also a Selectman and Justice of the Peace and eventually moved to Nashua where he was elected Mayor.

Although the company's first building burned to the ground during the first winter, it was soon rebuilt, and glassmaking was successfully continued. In 1849 it was listed in the *New England Mercantile Directory* as C. Curtis and Company, Black Glass Bottles, and by 1854 it was producing annually $2500 worth of bottles of various sizes and descriptions, according to Gould's *History*.

Scripture, Whiton and Curtis failed two years later and George L. Curtis from Windsor, Vermont, who was probably a relation of Calvin's took over the business. He had been employed by the firm as a distributing agent or shipper and, after taking B. F. Messer as a partner, continued the business under the old name of the Granite Glass Company. (They also used Messer and Curtis as a firm name.) It is of interest to note that Curtis also ran a store and built a large white house in the center of town. In 1858 the partnership of Messer and Curtis was dissolved, Messer sold out to his partner and Curtis carried on alone until 1862, when he left Stoddard. His leaving marked the end of the Granite Glass Company, and it is believed that the buildings were destroyed by fire in 1864.

Note: An interesting side-light is that apparently the two warehouses sold by Curtis in 1860 to Weeks and Gilson of the South Stoddard Glass Company were the same buildings erected by Foster in South Stoddard, having been assigned to Scripture, Whiton and Curtis after Foster failed in 1850.

The "Granite" made containers for wholesale liquors and patent medicines predominantly, producing half-pint (now very rare), pint and quart flasks with an eagle on each side. Other general products of the company included: Stoddard Lily Pad Pitchers, inkwells, jars, hats and various "off-blown" pieces.

Examples of flasks from this second factory at Mill Village will be found on pages 54 and 61.

About 1850, glassmaking really gathered momentum
when five men organized a new company. They were:
Luman Weeks, Almon Woods, Ebenezer A. Rice, Nicholas
Hilt and Frederick A. Gilson. They erected at the southeast
corner of the junction where Keene, Hillsboro Pike and the
Stoddard Road meet, a group of buildings including a warehouse, four tenements and a glass house. A store was added
two years later. Their choice of location may have been
influenced by the proximity of the Box Tavern, which was
owned by Weeks and Gilson, with Mr. Gilson as manager.

The new firm commenced operations under the name of
the South Stoddard Glass Company, but was later to produce
glass under the name Weeks and Gilson, and Weeks Glass
Works.

According to Child's *County Gazeteer and Directory* for
1885, Luman Weeks was born in Peru, New York in 1818;
he married Cynthia Pike of Marlow, New Hampshire and
moved to Stoddard in 1840. He was employed as a stage
driver from Marlow to Hancock until 1844 and from Stoddard
to Boston until 1850 when he went into the glass business,
in which he remained for twenty-three years, making 5½
gallon demi-johns and bottles and providing employment
for many people. Weeks was a selectman in Stoddard from
1864 to 1865, and in 1873 he moved to Keene. At least one
of Weeks' associates, it should be noted, had seen consider-
able experience in the glass industry. Nicholas Hilt had
been involved for twenty years or more in glassmaking at

Keene, but his Stoddard venture was short-lived, and after two years he returned to Keene.

Almon Woods and Nicholas Hilt bowed out of the business in 1852, and a year later Ebenezer Rice followed, thus leaving the business to Weeks and Gilson. This factory did not produce as great a volume as the Mill Village factory, but it ran successfully until 1873, when all glassmaking ceased in Stoddard.

The company's demise was due partly to the Depression following the Civil War and partly to customers' demands for clear glass, which could not be produced in Stoddard because of the silica in the soil of the area. Although the warehouse was full at this time, Weeks had no money with which to continue his shipping. A few years later the building was set on fire by persons unknown and burned to the ground, the fire also taking the tenements and the store.

The fortunes of the third glassworks also followed the rise and fall of the Saratoga Springs enterprises in New York State, since most of the mineral water bottles were supplied by Stoddard. Saratoga Springs had become famous as a resort and spa before the Civil War, and its mineral waters were in much demand. With the onset of the Civil War, the southern market, which was the major consumer of mineral spring water, ceased to exist. The Saratoga businesses collapsed upon the loss of this market and the glass factory fell into a severe financial decline.

The main output of Weeks' South Stoddard Glass Company consisted of the dark glass quart bottles for Saratoga Springs water. Among them were bottles embossed "High Rock Congress Spring Co." in reddish amber and olive-amber; and reddish amber bottles for the Star Spring Company with an embossed star in the center. The company also produced off-blown vases and jars for Kimball's Jaundice Bitters of Troy, New Hampshire in olive-amber.

At this writing, the author knows of only 14 bottles in existence with "Weeks and Gilson, So. Stoddard, N. H." embossed on the bottom.

·RING WATER BOTTLE, quart size, manactured by Weeks at South Stoddard, d embossed "High Rock Congress ʼring—C & W, Saratoga, N. Y." In the nter is the rock and above it "1787," e date of the Clarke and White Co.'s unding. On some examples the date as omitted. See also page 78.

About 1860, just before the Civil War, the last glassworks to be built in Stoddard was established by the sons of Joseph Foster at Mill Village. George Foster managed the business, while Charles and Wallace were glass-blowers. The youngest brother, Joseph, made wicker covers for carboys and demijohns. Just prior to 1868, Charles B. Barrett, a merchant of Boston bought out the Fosters. Barrett sold liquor and tobacco to finance the glassworks—his advertising stating that he was the only manufacturer of glass to sell his own wares and thus pass on to the customer the savings of an agent's commission.

The Foster boys had used the trade name, Granite Glass Works, and after the business was sold to Barrett, he called it the New Granite Glass Works. There is no evidence that Joseph Foster, Senior, now in his sixties, had any part in his sons' venture—although he reportedly had ties to the glass industries in South Lyndeborough and Cambridge, Mass.

This New Granite Glass Works made golden amber bottles. Their products included the deeply paneled jar with three panels on each side, cookie containers, fruit jars and flasks with its chief products the larger jars for household use.

They made three flasks which are rare and eagerly sought by collectors. These consist of a pint and a half-pint flask showing on the obverse side the United States flag ("Stoddard Flag Flasks") with thirteen stars and nine bars to the right, and on the reverse the inscription, "New Granite Glass Works, Stoddard, N. H." The other flask, which is extremely rare, is a half-pint and shows the flag with sixteen stars and thirteen bars, to the left instead of the right. Only two or three specimens of this flask are known. These flasks are usually amber and olive-amber bottle glass, and rarely olive-green, since these were the colors resulting from the nature of the sand which was secured solely from the local area. On the market, these bottles were used for whiskey.

The variety of these wares is shown by the list of products advertised by Charles Barrett, the new owner. It included: 15-gallon demi-johns, flasks and bottles for wine, soda,

GLASS MAKERS in the blowing room at the New Granite Glass Works. Only the young boy seems to have remained motionless for the photographer. From an old daguerreotype taken circa 1860, donated by John M. Foster, courtesy Keene Public Library

35

mineral water, ale, ink (inkwells, too), blacking, bay water, cologne, hair oil and patent medicines—plus every other conceivable type of bottle in black, and shades of amber.

Workers at this mill were greatly addicted (as were many other glassblowers in the country) to the "Cornucopia" design for half-pint, pint and quart bottles. A very rare bottle of this type exists with a "Cornucopia" on both sides, probably a product of a blower's experimentation with molten glass.

It was in this factory that the art of blowing amber glass in New Hampshire reached its peak.

In 1871, the New Granite Glass Works was struck by fire and burned to the ground. Surveying the damage at Mill Village, Barrett decided not to rebuild. Two years later—when Week's glass house at South Stoddard was threatened with insolvency, a last ditch effort was made to rescue it. The "expert," hired by the town to save the local industry, made herculean attempts. For nearly three months, he took three batches of molten glass a day and experimented with it, trying to produce clear glass. His failure spelled the doom of the Weeks company and for the Stoddard glass industry.

Appearances of temporary prosperity to the contrary, the glass industry in Stoddard never seems to have been able to gain a secure and profitable base. The constant shifts and reorganization of owners and partners in the four glass houses indicate that the companies were treading a thin line financially. Allowing for the free-wheeling business practices of the day, owners and managers seem to have come and gone with unusual rapidity. Even in the "boom" times of the 1860's, when the mills employed 800 people and produced $40,000 worth of glass annually, the profits must have been slim and the optimism short-lived. Of all the various proprietors of the glass houses, Luman Weeks persisted the longest—and to the end.

Indeed, in the face of so many obstacles, it seems remarkable that the Stoddard mills survived as long as they did. Aside from the inherent flaw in the local sand which rendered it impossible to produce the clear glass that had come into popular demand after the Civil War, the industry had to struggle with a host of other difficulties. Not the least of these was the inhospitable climate which forced the mills to shut down for nearly six months of the year. The remoteness of the industry from its markets, plus bad roads and inadequate transportation, were unquestionably a factor in the failure of Stoddard glassmaking. The railroad was not built to Stoddard until the 1880's—too late for the glassworks. After the Civil War the Stoddard mills were still relying upon a large laboring force to cut and cure timber (a year was required to age the wood), with which to fuel its furnaces—while more efficient competitive companies had switched to gas and coal. To an industry already beset be such seemingly insurmountable problems as these, the financial Panic of 1873 undoubtedly furnished the final blow.

4

The Making and the Makers of Glass
at Stoddard

THE SCENE at a typical glass works of the period in New England would show large groups of bustling workers in and around a factory building (usually hexagonal in shape) and two-storied wooden warehouses. The latter were removed sufficiently from the main building to guard against fire.

The factory building had a pyramid-shaped center with an open top to permit the intense heat to escape. Inside one might see groups of men making retorts for preparing glass and others putting the materials in condition for use. About the great furnace itself, almost at the melting point, sweltering mechanics would be dipping from the fiery contents various-sized red, wax-like globs of glass which they converted into bottles ranging from ink size to ten gallon demijohns. Then other workmen would take them as they were struck, tearing them away on sticks from the blowers' pipes to be placed in the great tempering ovens, from which they emerged ready for wickering or for the market.

Coming from several directions outside the factory building, one would probably see teams conveying large quantities of wood, for the furnaces and other materials for use about the works. Other teams, perhaps even bigger and more powerful, would bear away finished products or bring in supplies for trade and the subsistence of the families employed there. Probably as many men, if not more, were engaged in cutting and hauling timber for the furnaces, or in digging sand, as were actually making the glass.

Obviously the work was not dull and, indeed, it was occasionally quite dangerous. Modern safety standards were unheard of. Men were constantly exposed to burns and scorching from the quantities of molten glass, and fire was

BRICK once part of a glass furnace, discovered at the Stoddard "Box" site. The brick is amber and covered with a bluish tinge from the intense heat

an ever-present hazard in the furnace buildings—as testified by the record of destructive blazes during the thirty years the Stoddard Mills were operating. The danger was not confined to the furnaces. The record has it that one seventeen-year-old boy named Henry Whitman a native of Stoddard, was digging at the Granite Glass Company sandbank in March 1853, when the bank suddenly collapsed and an avalanche of sand buried the boy, killing him instantly.

Stoddard's chief fame and attraction does not lie so much in the commercial Stoddard pieces as it does in the "off-blown" pieces. In the custom of the time, the owner of the factory allowed the glassblowers at the end of the day to use the residue in the bottom of the melting pot to blow any pieces they desired for their own personal use. Because of this custom, many fine examples of the glassblower's art exist today in collections. In following his own whims, the glassblower of a century ago produced such interesting and rare pieces as vases, jugs, bowls, and witch's balls of diaphanous beauty. (And thus the term "whimseys" to describe these "off-blown" pieces).

Charles and Wallace Foster, two of the four Foster Brothers, were themselves adept glassblowers. And Weeks and Gilson, as well as Scripture, Whiton and Curtis had excellent glassblowers in their employ in the 1840's and 1850's. Among the best were the Cutter brothers and the McClure brothers. Two others were Horatio Smith and Matt Johnson. Smith at one time owned the famous Hancock Tavern near Faneuil Hall in Boston, and after leaving Stoddard, he followed the Gold Rush west to California in the 1850's. He died in Sacramento.

"Mighty Matt" Johnson was an Englishman who had

LILY PAD PITCHER, an example of Stoddard "off-blown" work, probably by Matt Johnson. The pitcher, which was used as a milk jug, is amber in color, eight inches high, and has four lily pads applied around the bottom. Photograph by Frank Kelly, courtesy Currier Museum, Manchester, N. H.

first come to this country to work in the glass factories of southern New Jersey. At Stoddard he was known for his practice of the "South Jersey technique." Equipped with strong lungs and skilled hands, he was considered one of the experts in the field of "off-blown" glass. He took particular pride in blowing special pieces for visitors to the Stoddard Works, such as amber pitchers, vases and bottles. Matt Johnson is remembered best for the unique "Lilypad" pitchers and tiny inverted blue and amber Uncle Sam hats.

A tale of this period has survived to show how "whimseys" were made, treasured and handed down. The story goes that a young boy named David Brainard Tyrrell, born in Hinsdale, New Hampshire, enlisted at the age of sixteen in the Union Army, where he served as one of the youngest drummer boys in the Yankee cause in the Civil War. Surviving the war, he returned to Hinsdale and in 1872 visited the Stoddard Glass Factory. After a grand tour of these facilities, he asked for a souvenir. One of the glassblowers blew a sphere, commonly called a witch's ball, for him. In later years, Tyrrell lived at the home of "Grandma" Bessie Apted, who took in elderly boarders. Wearing a long white beard and spending the greater part of his time sitting in the kitchen with two cats on his lap, he would relate his adventures in the Great Rebellion to the other boarders. When Tyrrell died in 1937, he left his "Stoddard Ball" to Agnes Williams, a young woman who was then living with Mrs. Apted. She still has this glass in her possession today and regards it as a rare item because of its interesting story and background.

The skilled glassblowers and hundreds of other workers suddenly found themselves left out of work when Barrett's

WITCH'S BALL, a whimsey piece, amber in color and four inches in diameter, was blown in 1872 and given to David B. Tyrrell, who was visiting Stoddard at the time. Tyrrell left it to a lady in Stoddard, who owns it to this day.

New Granite Glass Works burned in 1871 and when Weeks closed his plant at South Stoddard in 1873. Some of the families, most of them natives of Stoddard, stayed on to eke out a living as best they could, lumbering or farming. But most of the men, especially the trained glassmakers, moved on. Some migrated to Redford and Corning in New York State and other glass manufacturing centers. Others were undoubtedly drawn to the South Lyndeborough Glass Company, less than twenty-five miles distant. This firm had been started in 1866, and Charles Barrett owned a substantial share in it. The Fosters and their descendants found a successful outlet for their skills in the midwest. A. M. Foster, a great-grandson of the original Joseph Foster who had founded the Stoddard glass industries, became president of a glassworks in Indiana. The Foster-Forbes Glass Company of Marion, Indiana continues today in the hands of the same family.

Many of the staid old-time residents of Stoddard did not mourn the passing of the industry nor the exodus of the glassworkers. Some of the best glassblowers and their apprentices were German or Irish. There were plenty of young bachelors among them, whose "foreign ways" and boisterous living habits did not endear them to some of their conservative Yankee neighbors. For thirty years the taverns—the Central at Mill Village and "The Box" at South Stoddard—did a thriving business. The Box Tavern, a large rambling wooden building, was the hub of activity in the area, as a lively gathering place as well as a lodging house for scores of glassworkers, their friends and families. Hundreds knew its hospitality and many called it home until it was leveled by fire after the mills closed in the 1870's.

44

5

Identifying Stoddard Glass

"How can you tell it is Stoddard?" If the item is not *marked* Stoddard or *marked* by a name known to be connected with Stoddard, such as Weeks, Foster or Farley, no one can *prove* it is Stoddard. However, we can assume if many pieces of the same kind of bottle were dug at the site of the Mills—and conformed to other known aspects of Stoddard Glass, in color, style, type or lip or bottom and mold marks—that is probably Stoddard. We may attribute some value also to the likelihood that bottles dug in this area are more apt to be Stoddard than a bottle from Connecticut or further away, since transportation facilities at that time were extremely inadequate.

How can you tell if it's not Stoddard? Stoddard did *not* make:

1. Turn mold bottles
2. Clear glass
3. Two mold fifths
4. Dishes, bowls or glasses (not for general production, though some

were made by the glassblowers as off-blown pieces or whimseys)

5. Quilted pieces

There is no set rule for identifying Stoddard glass. The author has based her identification of pieces discussed in this text on the comparative method. Numerous fragments, bottoms, tops, etc. which were dug at the Mill sites have been used to compare pontil marks, necks and color. Due to specific impurities in the sand in the Stoddard area, Stoddard glass seems to have a color all its own—a dark olive amber. Of course, many Stoddard pieces are marked. There were "Farley's" inks, which came in various sizes and were made specially for Farley's Store located in Marlow, New Hampshire, just a few miles from Stoddard.

Pint and quart flasks are to be found, reading "Granite Glass Co.", embossed in three lines, and on the reverse side, "Stoddard, N. H.", embossed in two lines.

Another marked Stoddard product was the medicine bottle reading, "Kimball's Jaundice Bitters, Troy, New Hampshire."

One (quart size) bottle is marked "Weeks and Gilson, So. Stoddard, N. H." Another (fifth size) says "Weeks Glass Works."

Quart size bottles also exist marked "Fs" (upper and lower case). This is assumed to stand for Foster—Joseph Foster, the first man to make bottles in Stoddard.

Many of the spring water bottles made for Saratoga at Stoddard were embossed:

High Rock Congress Spring, C. & W., Saratoga, N. Y. (mountain embossed in center)

Star Spring Co., Saratoga, N. Y. (star embossed in center)
Congress & Empire Spring Co., Saratoga, N. Y. (rear has E embossed in center)
Hathorn Spring, Saratoga, N. Y.
Middletown Healing Springs, Grays and Clark, Middletown, Vt.
Clarke & White, New York (C embossed in center)
Clarke & White, New York (pint)
Clarke & White, New York (no letter embossed in center)
D. A. Knowlton, Saratoga, N. Y.

An important point to keep in mind when attempting the identification of a difficult specimen is that molds were sometimes exchanged between glass houses, such as the Keene and Stoddard houses of New Hampshire. (It will be remembered that glassmaking at Keene continued until 1855.) Indeed, often as a new design was launched by a bottle house, it would be openly copied by other glass houses, thus complicating the collector's job of identifying by shape.

In this connection, there is no evidence that Stoddard ever produced the so-called "blown three-mold glass." I mention the subject here only because among some collectors the false notion persists, even to the present day, that the Stoddard glasshouses manufactured glass of this type.

"Blown three-mold" is something of a misnomer. The term refers specifically to a less expensive method of imitating cut glass. By this method the glass was blown into iron or wooden molds, which had cut-glass patterns carved on them, attempting to imitate the real article. It came to be called "blown three-mold" because most of the molds were made in three parts, but, in fact, two and four-part molds

47

were also used. The resulting glassware had high-relief patterns, but instead of the sharp line of cut glass, the images were rounder and more diffused.

The "blown three-mold" method was developed by American glassmakers in the early 1800's in an effort to imitate and fill the demand for English and Irish cut glass, which was then very difficult to import due to the Napoleonic Wars. Manufacturers in New England and the Midwest produced a wide variety of "blown three-mold" wares, mostly of clear glass and sometimes colored, in numerous designs and sizes. But by the time the Stoddard industry began in the early 1840's, "blown three-mold" glass was on the wane and had lost much of its popular appeal.

To further mislead the novice collector, the specialized term "blown three-mold" is apt to be confused with other bottles which happened to be made from three-part molds. The two are not necessarily the same! In other words, because a bottle was made from a three-part mold does not mean it was produced by the so-called "blown three-mold" process. In *Early American Bottles,* Van Rensselaer points out that "too often . . . collectors and dealers seeing three-mold marks on a piece of pressed ware assume that the article belongs to this early nineteenth century American blown table ware [i.e. 'blown three-mold glass'] . . . Mold marks alone are not sufficient for identification."

Thus, as mentioned earlier in this chapter, a combination of factors must be considered in identifying Stoddard ware —or any other particular type of glass. While "blown three-mold" glass is a desirable collector's item, there is no concrete evidence known to the present writer—nor to numerous authorities in the field—that any "blown three-mold" pieces have ever been unearthed at the sites of the Stoddard mills.

Glass, like other art forms, can provide false clues for the collector. But it doesn't require an expert to recognize the signs which can unmistakeably identify Stoddard products. Once the basic characteristics have been learned, even the novice can unearth a rare piece. It may be at a country auction, in a jumble shop, an attic or none of these places at all. Even an unsuccessful search can be rewarding in pleasurable anticipation of a find. The writer has combed the woods around the abandoned site of old Stoddard School No. 1, where literally dozens of inkwells are said to lie. They were propelled there, according to a 73-year-old town selectman from South Stoddard, by the ends of rulers wielded by generations of schoolboys long before the missile age.

A single one of these Stoddard "inks" has a value today that would buy the family groceries for a month. None has as yet been found, by this writer or anyone else known to her, but there is always hope. And it is hope that keeps collectors on the trail of Stoddard glass, wherever it leads.

Glassware Photographed

THREE FLASKS

1. Cornucopia pattern, half-pint. Sheared top. On reverse side *below* is urn with six panels. 5½". Amber.
2. Unembossed horseshoe type, with tapered applied lip. Rough pontil. The type that had metal covering on bottom part of bottle. Sometimes called a "pocket flask". *Below:* Same flask seen from bottom. Amber.
3. "Scott and Byron" historical, half-pint. Sheared top and ribbed sides with rough pontil. No embossing except pictures. Reverse seen *below*. 5¾". Amber.

Two Flasks

1. STODDARD, N. H.—pint. Double laid-on ring lip. Sloping shoulders. Reverse side embossed GRANITE GLASS CO. Amber.

2. GRANITE GLASS CO.—pint. Tapered applied lip, sloping shoulders. Reverse side embossed STODDARD, N. H. Almost identical to its companion, except for lip. Amber.

THREE FLASKS

1. Double Eagle—quart. STODDARD, N. H. embossed on oval. Sheared top, open pontil. On some bottles of this type, Stoddard is spelled with only one "d"—STODARD. Amber.
2. Double Eagle—half-pint. Unembossed oval beneath. Sheared top, open pontil—6". Blood amber.
3. Double Eagle—pint. Unembossed oval beneath. Sheared top, open pontil. 6". Amber.

Three Flasks

1. Unembossed horseshoe, half-pint. Crude laid-on ring collar, improved pontil. 6¼". Amber.
2. Unembossed patent type, pint. Dimple in center on one side only. Double laid-on ring collar. Improved pontil. 7¼". Amber.
3. PATENT, embossed pint. Dimple in center on one side. Double laid-on ring collar. 7¼". Amber.

FIVE FLASKS, PATENT TYPE
with double laid-on rings and improved pontils.

1. Unembossed, pint. 7½". Amber.
2. Unembossed, half-pint. 6½". Amber.
3. Unembossed, quart. 9". Honey Amber.
4. PATENT embossed half-pint. 6½". Blood Amber.
5. PATENT embossed pint. 7½". Amber.

FOUR WHISKEYS
All Embossed on Bottom

1. WEEKS GLASS WORKS embossed on bottom, fifth, with original label: "Old Cognac—James Hennessey". Three-part mold. 11½". Dark Amber.

2. "Fs". Fifth. Probably a Foster product. Tapered applied lip, improved pontil. 11½". Burgundy. Very Rare.

3. WEEKS AND GILSON—STODDARD, N. H. Quart. Three-part mold, tapered applied lip, improved pontil. 12". Blood Amber.

4. WEEKS GLASS WORKS—Fifth. Three-part mold, tapered applied lip, improved pontil. 11½". Amber.

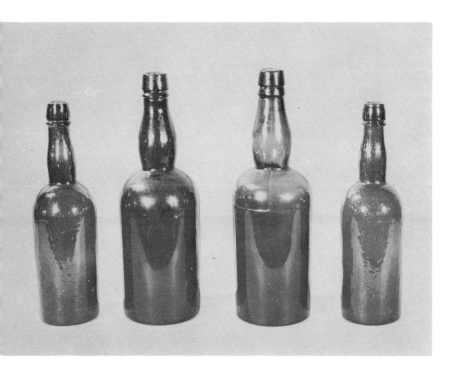

FOUR LADY'S LEG WHISKEYS, UNEMBOSSED

1. Pint Tapered applied lip, 3-part mold, improved pontil. 8″. Amber.
2. Quart Tapered applied lip, 3-part mold, dot on base. 9″. Olive-Amber.
3. Quart Tapered applied lip, 3-part mold, dot on base. 9″. Amber.
4. Pint Tapered applied lip, 3-part mold, improved pontil.

THREE STODDARD STUBBYS, UNEMBOSSED BEERS

1. Half-pint Tapered applied lip, 3-part mold, improved pontil. 6½".
   Amber.
2. Half-pint Tapered applied lip, 3-part mold, improved pontil. 6½".
   Olive-Amber.
3. Half-pint Tapered applied lip, 3-part mold, improved pontil. 6½".
   Burgundy.

TWO WHISKEYS AND A FLASK

1. Unembossed Quart. Applied tapered top. Numerous bubbles or "tears",
    3-part mold, improved pontil. 10½". Honey-Amber.
2. STODDARD, N. H. Embossed flask, pint. Embossing on reverse is GRAN-
    ITE GLASS CO. Double laid-on ring top, open pontil. 7½". Amber.
3. Unembossed Quart. Same as example at left, but color is Blood-Amber.

FOUR MEDICINES, EMBOSSED

1. OPODELDOC LIQUID. Cylindrical, thin flared lip, open pontil. 4½". Amber.
2. GIBB'S BONE LINIMENT. Six panels, tapered applied lip, open pontil. 5¾". Olive-Amber.
3. DR. HARTSHORNS MEDICINE on inset panel on one side. Rectangular, rounded shoulders, applied ring lip, improved pontil. 5¾". Dark Amber.
4. SEAVER'S JOINT AND NERVE LINIMENT. Cylindrical, thin flared lip, squared shoulders, open pontil. 4⅛". Amber.

Octagonal Medicine (Two Sides)

1. HOLMAN'S NATURE'S GRAND RESTORATIVE. Thin applied lip, rough pontil, 6¾", olive-amber. J. B. HOLMAN, PROP. is embossed on the narrow side, seen *at right*.

Two Octagonal Medicines (Also on opposite page)

1. HOWARD'S VEGETABLE. Thin applied lip and short neck, rough pontil. Thin panels on ends. Reverse embossing on *opposite page*. 7¼". Olive-amber.

2. Octagonal medicine on its side, similar to its companion. Rough pontil, olive-amber. Embossed side shown on *opposite page*.

Two Octagonal Medicines (Continued)

1. CANCER AND CANKER SYRUP is the embossing on the reverse of the HOWARD'S VEGETABLE seen on page 64.

2. N. WOOD, PORTLAND, ME. is the embossing on the side of the other bottle shown opposite. Note the applied tapered top, which gives it slightly more height than the other octagonal example.

SODA (Two Sides)

1. Two views of DR. TOWNSEND'S SARSAPARILLA, ALBANY, N. Y.
Square, with chamfered corners, embossed on three sides.
Four mold dots on each side. Long tapered collar lip. 9¾".
Dark Amber.

THREE MEDICINES

1. Unembossed three-part mold, similar to "stubby" except for very short neck with double tapered lip. Very rough pontil. 6¾". Amber.

2. Unembossed medicine (or whiskey). Quart. Like example on page 58, with "Weeks and Gilson" embossing, except for unusual long tapered lip. 11½". Amber.

3. J. C. LAUGHTON & CO., BOSTON. Three-part mold, dimple on bottom, long tapered collar with ring on lower edge. Same shape as "Lady's Legs" (page 59) except for its straight neck. 9½". Amber.

Medicine and Bitters

1. Unembossed medicine. Flared top, open pontil. 5". Amber.
2. KIMBALL'S JAUNDICE BITTERS with TROY, N. H. embossed on reverse. Eight-sided, short tapered lip, sloping shoulders. 7". Amber.
3. Unembossed 3-part mold. Pint. Long neck and tapered lip with ring under it. Color is definitely green. This bottle was dug at the site of the Stoddard Box factory, along with many others, some broken; there was also slag of the same green. (So Stoddard *did* make some green bottles!)

BLACKING BOTTLES

1. Blacking bottle, (also used for shoe polish). Square with open pontil and sheared top. Olive-amber.
2. An identical blacking bottle, on its side to show open pontil.
3. Blacking bottle. Long neck with double laid-on ring, sloping shoulders. Similar to "Dr. Jewett's, Rindge, N. H. Bitters." Color: green with bluish tinge half way up bottle.

EIGHT-SIDED FARLEY'S INKS, ALL EMBOSSED

1. Horizontal embossing on two panels. Sharply rounded shoulders, short straight neck and sheared top. Rough pontil. 1¾". Amber.
2. Same as first, except for rolled lip. 1¾". Amber.
3. Similar to first, except shoulder slopes more gradually to neck. 2". Dark Amber.
4. Vertical embossing on two panels. Thin flared lip. 3". Honey Amber.
5. Similar to fourth example, except for slightly curved neck. 4". Honey Amber.

THREE INKS, UNEMBOSSED

1. Master Ink. Three-part mold, with pouring spout. 7½". Amber.
2. Umbrella Ink. Octagonal, with rough pontil. Amber.
3. Master Ink. Three-part mold, with tapered top and no pouring spout. Amber.

FIVE INKS

1. Master Ink, pint. Pouring spout, long tapered collar with small ring beneath. Three-part mold, dimple on bottom. 7½″. Amber.
2. Umbrella Ink. Sixteen-sided, with short neck, sheared top and rough pontil. Amber.
3. Master Ink. Quart. Pouring spout with long tapered lip. Three-part mold, dimple on bottom. Amber.
4. Umbrella Ink. Eight-sided, full of bubbles, and has a brass top. Rough pontil. Amber.
5. Umbrella Ink. Eight-sided, sheared top, open pontil. Amber. Most popular of Stoddard umbrella inks.

THREE SPRING WATERS, EMBOSSED

1. MISSISQUOI SPRINGS with large "A". Quart with long tapered collar and
   laid-on ring. Occasionally has Indian Princess' head embossed on reverse, and if so, very rare. 9½". Dark Amber.

2. MAGNETIC SPRING, HENNIKER, N. H. Quart, similar to first example. Dark
   Amber.

3. HATHORN SPRING. Quart, two-part mold, with collar and ring similar
   to others. Dark Amber.

CLARKE & WHITE SPRING WATER BOTTLES

1. CLARKE & WHITE, NEW YORK. Quart with long tapered collar and ring beneath. Improved pontil. Olive-amber.

2. Same as first, except for large "C" and more pronounced embossing. Olive-amber.

CLARKE & WHITE SPRING WATER BOTTLES

1. CLARKE & WHITE, NEW YORK. Pint size with short neck. Olive-amber.
2. Same embossing as first example. Quart with sloping shoulder and short straight neck. Olive-amber.

THREE SPRING WATERS, EMBOSSED

1. MIDDLETOWN HEALING SPRINGS, GRAYS & CLARK, MIDDLETOWN, VT. Quart, with long tapered collar and laid-on ring. 9½". Honey-Amber.
2. CONGRESS & EMPIRE SPRING CO., SARATOGA, N. Y. with large "E" in center. Of same size and shape as first example, but color is Olive-green.
3. MIDDLETOWN HEALING SPRINGS. Identical to first example, but it has many whittle marks and color is Amber.

THREE SPRING WATERS, EMBOSSED

1. D. A. KNOWLTON, SARATOGA, N. Y. Quart. Long tapered lip with ring beneath. Amber.

2. HATHORN SPRING, SARATOGA, N. Y. Pint with tapered collar and ring. (Note other example for same firm, page 73) Amber.

3. CONGRESS & EMPIRE SPRING CO., SARATOGA, N. Y. with large "C" in center. Quart, almost identical in shape to first example. Other bottle for same company on page 76. Olive-amber.

Two Spring Waters, Embossed

1. HIGH ROCK CONGRESS SPRING CO., C & W, SARATOGA, N. Y. with rock embossed in center. Quart, with long tapered collar and laid-on ring. Amber.

2. SARATOGA SPRING with Star in center. Note reversed "S" in Spring. Almost identical to preceding example. Amber.

Two Spring Waters, Embossed

1. CONGRESS & EMPIRE SPRING CO. - HOTCHKISS & SONS, NEW YORK-SARATOGA, N. Y. with large "C" in center. Pint with same style top as others. (With all the embossing, there is scarcely any space left.) Amber.

2. MAGNETIC SPRING, HENNIKER, N. H. Quart in same style as two examples opposite. Other bottle for same company, on page 73, is of darker hue. Amber.

SNUFF AND MEDICINE BOTTLES

1. Medicine. Flared top, open pontil. 4¼". Amber.
2. Snuff with original label LORILLARD'S MACCOBOY SNUFF on broad side. Bottle is actually octagonal, with round shoulders and very short flared lip. Other snuffs of this type were known to have been made at Stoddard. 4". Amber.
3. Medicine. Short tapered lip, open pontil. 4¼". Amber.
4. *Below:* Snuff bottle, bottom view, showing label on reverse and the embossed "W" on bottom. The letter probably stood for Weeks.

Medicine

Unembossed medicine (or bitters) with
curved shoulders and round arched panel
on each side to accommodate paper labels.
Short neck, tapered lip, rough pontil. 7½".
Amber.

PICKLE

Pickle, with eight projecting curved panels. Laid-on ring for lip. Improved pontil. 8″. Amber.

Three Household Bottles, Unembossed

1. Medicine (or whiskey). Quart, with long tapered collar. Same type as WEEKS AND GILSON bottle, page 58, but without embossing. Dark Amber.
2. Demijohn, very small. Long tapered collar, open pontil. Amber.
3. Food jar. Three-part mold, round shoulders, with wide mouth and thick flared rim. Amber.

FREE-BLOWN DEMIJOHN

Free-blown bottle with open pontil and
applied tapered lip. 13″. Honey Amber.

Two Demijohns

1. Three-part mold demijohn with iron pontil and tapered lip. 13½". Burgundy.
2. Three-part mold demijohn with improved pontil and tapered lip. 13½". Amber.

FIVE DEMIJOHNS OF VARIED SIZES

1. Demijohn (or cylinder) bottle. Two piece mold with rounded shoulders, long applied tapered lip, dimple on bottom. Base diameter 7", height 19". Burgundy.
2. Free-blown demijohn, or cylinder, with applied lip and rough pontil. Base diameter 8½", Height 17". Amber.
3. Free-blown, with applied tapered lip, rough pontil. Base diameter 7", height 15". Amber.
4. Three-part mold, applied top, improved pontil. Base diameter 6", height 14". Red-Amber.
5. Free-blown, with applied tapered lip, open pontil. Base diameter 5", height 12". Amber.

Mug, Off-Blown

Mug, blown into a piece of stove pipe, which covers the bottom two-thirds of the piece. Square and circular openings were cut in the metal to form convex patterns of glass. Rough pontil, applied handle. 6¼″. Amber.

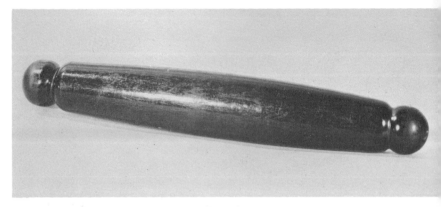

ROLLING PIN, OFF-BLOWN

This solid glass rolling pin has a broken pontil on one end, is 16″ long and has a diameter of 2½″. Dark Amber.

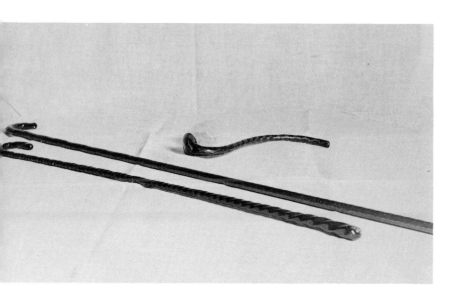

PIPE AND TWO CANES, OFF-BLOWN

1. Small cane of solid glass with twisted pattern. Diameter about ½″, length 18″. Amber.
2. Large cane, solid glass. Twisted pattern is less pronounced. Diameter ⅝″, length 24″. Amber.
3. Pipe. Curved solid stem with twisted pattern and clear glass bowl. Amber.

CHRISTMAS BALL AND TWO WITCH'S BALLS

1. Large Witch Ball. Amber.
2. Small Witch Ball. Amber.
3. Ball for Christmas tree ornament. Amber.

Saddle Flask

An off-blown saddle flask which was usually covered with wicker or leather and was carried by a rider on horseback. 8″. Honey-amber.

BOWLER HAT

This small off-blown hat may have been used
as a toothpick holder. 2½″. Amber.

Other Products
Attributed to the Stoddard Mills

FLASKS

Double-Eagle embossed on oval "So. Stoddard, N. H.".
Sheared top, open pontil. 8″. Amber.

Double-Eagle embossed on oval "Stoddard". Sheared top.
open pontil. 6″. Amber.

Unembossed Patent-type, quart, laid-on ring top. 9″. Amber.

Unembossed Patent-type, Pint, laid-on ring top. 7¼″. Amber.

Unembossed Patent-type, Half-pint, laid-on ring top. 6½″.
Amber.

SPRING WATERS

"Star Spring Co.", embossed star on bottle. Pint. Amber.

"Guilford Mineral Spring Water, Guilford, Vt." Embossed
in circle "G M S W". Diamond outline around entire embossing.

WHISKEYS AND BEERS (All cylindrical with improved pontils)

Stubby. 6½". Green.

Fifth. 11½". Amber.

Fifth. 11½". Olive-amber.

Fifth. 11½". Burgundy.

Fifth. 11½". Light-amber.

Quart. 11½". Amber.

Pint. 8". Olive-amber.

Lady's Leg. Burgundy.

INKS

Farleys Ink (not pictured). Pint and Quart size, similar to 4".

Master Ink. Cylinder shape, quart size, three-part mold, applied top, with and without pouring spouts. Amber.

MEDICINES

Plain unembossed medicines ranging in height from 2" to 6½".

Cylinder shaped, flared or applied top, long tapered, open pontil.

EMBOSSED MEDICINES AND BITTERS

Chapman's Genuine No. 4, Salem St., Boston. Chamfered corners, short tapered collar.

R. Dunster, London. Half-pint square bottle with flattened corners

Forbes & Co., Chatham Square, N. Y. Oil Blacking

Huntington's Golden Tonic Bitters

Dr. Huntington's Golden Tonic Bitters, Portland, Maine

Dr. Stephen Jewett's Celebrated Pulmonary Elixer, Rindge, N. H.

J. Leavitt. Embossing across shoulder of pint size cylinder shaped bottle

Liquid Cathartic and Family Physic, Lowell, Mass.

J. W. Pollard. Embossed in crescent panel in front, sloped shoulders, flared top, 8½″ high

C. A. Richards, 99 Washington St., Boston. Similar in shape to "Dr. Townsend" bottle, page 66

G. W. Stone Vegetable Liquid Cathartic, Lowell, Mass.

OFF-BLOWN PIECES

Footed Bowl. Lily pad decoration. 6″. Dark reddish amber.

Footed Bowl. Small foot, bell shaped. 5⅞″. Deep reddish amber.

Deep Footed Bowl. Large foot, straight sides. 7¾". Dark reddish amber.

Deep Bowl. Blown in bottle mold. 5⅞". Pale amber.

Large Bowl for skimming milk. 13½" wide. Amber.

Bowl. 6". Amber

Sugar Bowl and Cover. Heavy. Diameter of foot approximately 4⅜". Open wing-type handles, domed top with knob. 7⅝". Olive-amber.

Sugar Bowl. Matches small 4" amber pitcher (below), witch's ball for cover. Amber.

Pitcher. Applied handle. Matching sugar bowl above. 4". Amber.

Pitcher. Applied handle. 6". Amber.

Pitcher. Applied handle. 9". Amber.

Pitcher. Miniature. 2". Amber.

Pitcher. Applied handle. 8". Olive-amber.

Preserve Jar. Small barrel shaped, flared top. 6½". Olive-amber.

Preserve Jar. Flared top. 8 5/16". Golden amber.

Basket. Similar to hat on page 92. Applied handle. About 2½". Amber.

Pinch bottle (flask or perfume).

Paperweights. Turtle or shell shaped. Three sizes: 6½, 4¼, and 3″. Amber

Spitoon. Amber

Trumpet-shaped Whimsey.

Insulator. Pilgrim hat shape. 3″. Dark amber.

Insulator. Dome top with single ridge near base. 2½″. Amber.

Glossary

Applied lip: the turned sloping edge at the neck, put on after the bottle was formed; often only a ring of glass trailed carelessly around the neck opening.

Black glass: dark, olive green glass, the color deepened by the thickness of the glass; made c. 1815-1875.

Blob top: the thick rounded lip on soda bottles and mineral water bottles.

Blown in mold: the process by which the gather of glass was blown into a mold to take the shape of the mold. The lip on the bottle was usually added later, and the bottom sometimes had open pontil scars.

Canteen flask: A flat round-shaped flask, resembling a military canteen, made c. 1815-1825. Similar to early concentric ring historical flask.

Carboy: large bottle with curved-out sides used to ship spirits and acids; usually it was encased in wicker. Larger than a demi-john.

Chestnut: An irregular, free-blown, shaped bottle, resembling a chestnut—especially if the sides were flattened. Sizes from ⅛ pint to about 2 quarts; colors were usually olive green, olive amber, and amber.

Chip mold: see Whittle marks.

Commemorative flask: made to commemorate an historical event.

Demijohn: Large straight-sided bottles which were used for shipping.

Dip-mold: An open top, one-piece mold.

Flared lip: Openings on older bottles which were spread outward to strengthen them.

Free-blown glass: Glass blown without the use of a mold; also called hand-blown.

Gather: a glob of molten glass at the end of a blowpipe.

Historical flask: A broad term covering flasks depicting historical events in America from about 1815 to 1880; it can include pictorial, portrait and commemorative flasks.

Improved pontil: The iron or graphite rod used to hold the bottom of a molten bottle during finishing, and which left a concave mark in the glass, usually with reddish or blackish tinges. Also called a graphite pontil or iron pontil.

Kick-up: a coneshaped indentation on the bottom of some bottles, achieved by placing the still semi-molten glass in a mold in which there is a convex piece of wood. Also called "push-up."

Laid-on ring: A bead of glass trailed around the neck of a bottle to reinforce it.

Lady's leg: A bottle with a curving neck; for example, a bitters bottle.

Master ink: A large bottle from which ink wells are filled.

Molded glass: Glass fastened with the use of a mold.

Off-blown: Glassware blown by glass blowers for their own enjoyment or personal use, usually at the end of the day after work was done. Sometimes called "off-hand pieces" or "whimseys."

Open pontil: a rough scar left at bottom of bottle; of earlier date than improved pontil.

Pictorial flask: a term referring to such pieces as Double Eagle, Eagle Cornucopia, and Cornucopia-Basket of Fruit flasks; made between 1780-1870.

Portrait flask: bottles carrying likenesses of presidents and other notables, such as Lafayette, Webster, Sir Walter Scott, Lord Byron and others; made c. 1820-1850.

Pontil, punty rod or puntee: An iron or steel rod used for fashioning the molten glass, to which it is attached by a small blob of glass first gathered on the rod.

Pontil scar: The mark remaining when the pontil rod is removed; the shape of the scars fall into several types: tubular, broken stem, raw-line, rough, and open.

Sheared top: The top of a bottle fire polished and cut off.

Sick glass: Glass which has deteriorated or has superficial decay—for which there is no cure.

Shoo-fly flask: A bottle narrower at the base than at the shoulder; sometimes called "casket" or "ribbon" flasks. Made c. 1890-1910.

Tears: Air bubbles imprisoned in the glass.

Violin flask: More heart-shaped than violin shaped; also called "scroll." Made c. 1845-1870.

Whimsey: see off-blown.

Whittle marks: Marks left on a bottle from the imperfections in a hand-carved wooden mold; sometimes caused by glass that was too cool at the time it was placed in the mold.

Reference Sources

Antiques. "Dispelling the Stoddard Myth" by Helen A. McKearin. August 1937

——————. "Keene, New Hampshire" by Harry Hall White. June 1927

——————. "Stoddard Glass" by Lura Watkins Woodside. August 1933

Bates, Virginia & Chamberlain, Beverly. *Antique Bottle Finds in New England.* Peterborough, N. H., 1968

Child, Hamilton. *Gazeteer of Cheshire County, N. H.* Syracuse, N. Y., 1885

Christianson, Erwin. *Index of American Design.* New York, 1950.

Glass Blowing: A Manual of Basic Techniques. Hellertown, Pa., 1956

Gould, Isaiah. *History of Stoddard, New Hampshire.* 1854. (Republished 1970).

Granite State Magazine. "First Glass Blowing in America" by C. B. Heald. January 1907.

Hopkins, Carl W. and Mildred E., Glass Collection, Historical Society of Cheshire County (catalog). This fine collection is open to the public at Keene, N. H.

Keene, N. H. Directory, 1831

Manchester Union-Leader. "Flasks Have Value" by C. W. Chisholm.

McKearin, George S. and Helen. *American Glass.* New York, 1941, 1968

New England Mercantile Directories. Boston, 1849 and subsequent years.

Stoddard, N. H., Annual Town Reports.

Upper Ashuelot: A History of Keene, New Hampshire. Keene, 1968

Van Renssalaer, Stephen. *Early American Bottles and Flasks,* privately printed, 1926

Index

Note: Embossings are printed in SMALL CAPITALS.

Olive-amber glass, 19, 28, 32, 33, 35, 94, 96; illus., 59, 60, 62-64, 69, 74-77
OPODELOC LIQUID, illus., 62
Owens, Michael J., 24

Paperweights, 97
Patent-type bottles, 30, 36, 93; illus., 56, 57
Peterborough, N. H., 16, 17, 19
Pickle bottle, 82
Pike, Cynthia, 31
Pipe (glass), illus., 89
Pitcher Mountain, 16
Pitchers, 30, 40-42, 96; illus., 41
Pocket flask, 53
Pollard, see J. W. Pollard
Portland, Maine, 64, 65, 95
Preserve Jars, 96
Pressed glass, 23

R. DUNSTER, LONDON, 95
Red-amber glass, 19, 28, 32, 95, 96; illus., 86; see also, blood-amber
Redford, N. Y., 44
Rice, Ebenezer A., 31, 32

Richardson family, 17
Rindge, N. H., 69, 95
Robinson, Enoch, 23
Rock, embossed, 46; illus., 33, 78
Rolling pin (glass), 88

Saddle flask; illus., 91
Salada, Roland, 12
Salem County, N. J., 23
Sanderson, Captain Jonathan, 17, 18
Sandwich Glass, 23
SARATOGA, N. Y., embossing, 32, 33, 46, 47, 74-79
Schoolcraft, Henry Rowe, 24, 27
"Scott and Byron" flask, 53
Scott, Sir Walter, embossed head, 53
Scripture, Gilman, 29, 30, 40
SEAVER'S JOINT AND NERVE LINIMENT, illus., 62
Shepard, Jean, 12
Smith, Horatio, 40
Snuff bottle, illus., 80
Soda bottles, 35; illus., 66
South Lyndeborough, N. H., 20, 25, 44

"W", embossing, illus., 80

Weeks and Gilson Co., 14, 26, 30-33, 46, 58, 67, 83; see also, South Stoddard Glass Co.

WEEKS AND GILSON, embossing, 33, 46, 67, 83; illus., 58

Weeks Glass Works, 31, 33, 36, 46, 58, 80

WEEKS GLASS WORKS, embossing, 46; illus., 58

Weeks, Luman, 26, 30-32, 36, 37, 40, 44, 45

Wentworth, Benning, 16

"Whimseys", 40, 42, 46, 94-96; see also, off-blown glass

Whiskey bottles, 24, 30, 34, 94; illus., 58, 59, 61; see also, flasks

Whitman, Henry, 40

Whitney, Nellie Louise, 15

Whiton, John Jr., 28-30, 40

Williams, Agnes, 42

Williams, Frederick A., Jr., 12

Williams, Joyce, 12

Window glass, 21, 23, 24

Windsor, Vt., 30

Wine bottles, 35

Wistar, Caspar, 23

Wistarberg glass, 23

Witch's balls, 40, 42, 96; illus., 43, 90

Wood, see N. Wood

Woods, Almon, 31, 32

NOTES

NOTES